NATIONAL GEOGRAPHIC

Ladders

GULF COAST

WHERE ON EARTH?

Read to find out about the geography and wildlife of the Gulf Coast.

Welcome to the Gulf Coast

by Sherri Patoka

You're standing on a beach watching waves splash toward you. Water from the Gulf of Mexico races past you and flows through tall grass. This flooding over the grass creates a **tidal marsh**. Tidal marshes make up a large part of this region and provide a home to many plants and animals.

This is the Gulf Coast of the United States. It's located along the Gulf of Mexico, a large body of water between the United States and Mexico. The Gulf is connected to the Atlantic Ocean, but it is mostly surrounded by land. So its water doesn't move around much, and it gets really salty.

The swamps of the Gulf Coast are home to many animals, including alligators and wading birds. Tangled trees called **mangroves** grow here, too.

This land isn't only swamp, though. Farther away from the ocean, the wet grassy marsh turns into hilly sand **dunes**. People on the Gulf Coast enjoy the sea and hot, sunny weather.

This Gulf Coast beach is in Baldwin County, Alabama.

Where on Earth?

THE GULF COAST

What is there to see on the Gulf Coast? Cool cities like New Orleans, weird wildlife, and natural history. Let's look at a few examples from states in the area.

Texas

The armadillo is the official state small mammal of Texas.

Legend has it that many Spanish treasure ships wrecked off the coast of South Padre Island. Treasure hunters still come there to search for gold and silver.

Texas was its own country from 1836 to 1845 before it became a U.S. state.

Louisiana

The city of Rayne has many frogs and frog-themed events. It is the world's "Frog Capital"!

The town of Jean Lafitte was a hideout for pirates in the 1800s.

The American Rose Center in Shreveport grows green roses called *Rosa monstrosa*.

Texas

< Armadillo

4

Mississippi

Gulfport calls itself the "Root Beer Capital of the World." A famous brand of root beer was started near there.

Visitors to the town of Flora can see petrified trees. An ancient river carried these trees to where they were covered with soil. Over time, the trees turned to stone.

While hunting in Mississippi, President Teddy Roosevelt refused to shoot a bear. That's how the Teddy bear got its name.

Alabama

Mail carriers bring the mail by boat in Magnolia Springs.

During flooding, Alabama's fire ants grab onto each other to form a raft so they can float!

Alabama has a giant statue of a boll weevil, an insect that destroyed the cotton crop in the early 1900s.

> Flamingo

Florida

Florida's pink flamingos get their color from eating shrimp.

Florida is the only place where alligators and crocodiles live in the same region.

The Seminole Indians of Florida have one word that means "a dry place in the swamp covered with many trees." It is *Opatishawockalocka* (OP-uh-TISH-uh-WOK-uh-LOK-uh).

Alabama

Mississippi

Louisiana

Florida

Check In How would you describe the land and water of the Gulf Coast?

Jellies and Other Creatures!

by Grace Coffey

At night, you might see glowing creatures in the Gulf of Mexico. They are called jellyfish, but they're not fish. Jellyfish can be transparent, or see-through, or they can be brown, pink, blue, or bright white. There are 200 different kinds of jellyfish.

Jellyfish have no spines. Between their outer and inner layers of skin is a jelly-like substance. That's why they're called jellyfish. They float through the water with ocean **currents** and move up and down by opening and closing their bell-shaped bodies. The ocean currents often wash jellyfish up on the beach with the tide.

A jellyfish has no brain. Instead, it uses a system of nerves, or fibers that send signals in the body, to detect light, feel the water, and find food. It uses its **tentacles**, or arms, to pick up tiny **organisms** to eat. But jellyfish also hunt bigger fish. If a fish touches a jellyfish's tentacles, it will get a poisonous sting. The poison stuns the fish, and the jellyfish pulls the fish into its mouth.

Jellyfish live in salty oceans near the coast. Very few have been found in fresh water. Usually jellyfish are tiny, from one inch to one foot long. But some jellies are giants—measuring seven feet long with tentacles as long as 200 feet!

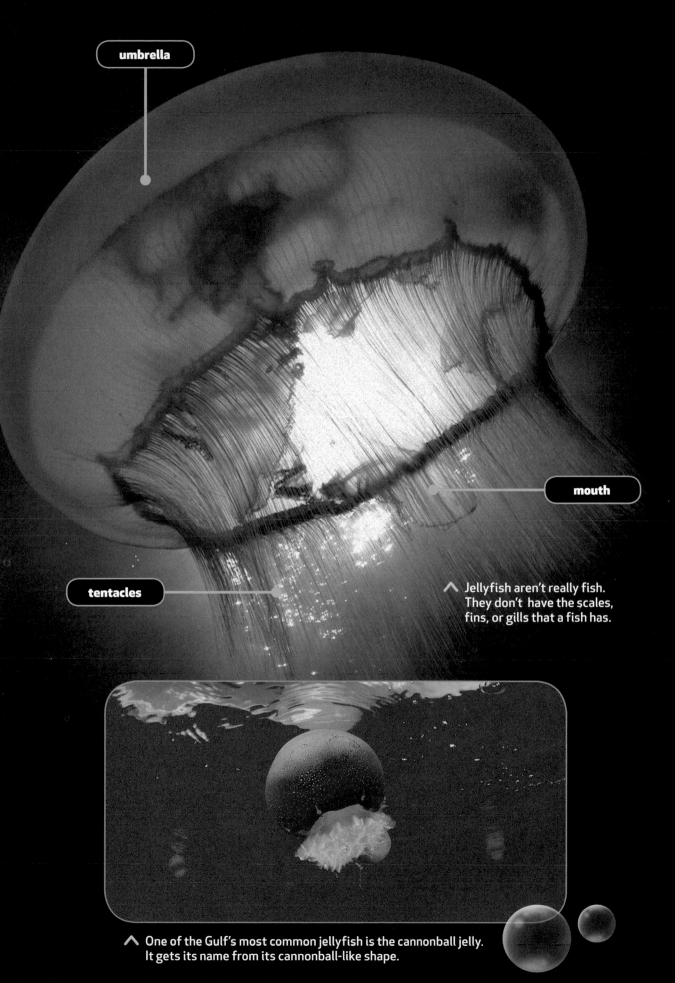

umbrella

mouth

tentacles

∧ Jellyfish aren't really fish.
They don't have the scales,
fins, or gills that a fish has.

∧ One of the Gulf's most common jellyfish is the cannonball jelly.
It gets its name from its cannonball-like shape.

Ouch, That Stings!

Watch out! Jellyfish won't attack humans, but they can be hard to see in the water. You could get stung by bumping into one.

A jellyfish's tentacles have stingers, like hooks. The stingers contain poison that shoots out when the jellyfish touches something. Even after a jellyfish dies, the tentacles remain dangerous. You can get stung by stepping on a dead jellyfish.

If you get stung by a jellyfish:

1. Leave the water. Tell a lifeguard or another adult.

2. Rinse the sting with vinegar or salt water. Rinsing can help stop the stinging. Do not use freshwater—that will just increase the stinging feeling.

3. With a stick or towel, scrape off any tentacles that are stuck to your skin.

4. If you have trouble breathing or feel sick or dizzy, get medical help immediately. Do the same if the redness spreads, or if you get bumps.

∧ The moon jellyfish is also common in the Gulf. How do you think it got its name?

It LOOKS Like a Jellyfish...

Along the Gulf Coast, you'll also find the Portuguese (POR-chuh-geez) man-of-war. Like the jellyfish, it has a rounded floating top and poisonous tentacles, but it's also WAY different. It's not even one single creature, but four creatures living as one. These strange creatures, called polyps (PAHL-uhps), can look very different.

The polyp at the top floats on the water and looks like a wartime sailing ship called a man-of-war. Other polyps make up the poisonous tentacles. The tentacles are usually about 30 feet long, but some can reach 150 feet or more. These deadly arms paralyze prey and carry it to the man-of-war's mouth, where another polyp digests it.

Men-of-war live in oceans around the world. You may see more than 1,000 floating together.

Portuguese men-of-war are also called bluebottles. The name comes from the blue color of the polyp that floats on the water.

Check In   Describe three facts that surprised you about jellyfish or men-of-war.

All in a Day's Work

by Brett Gover

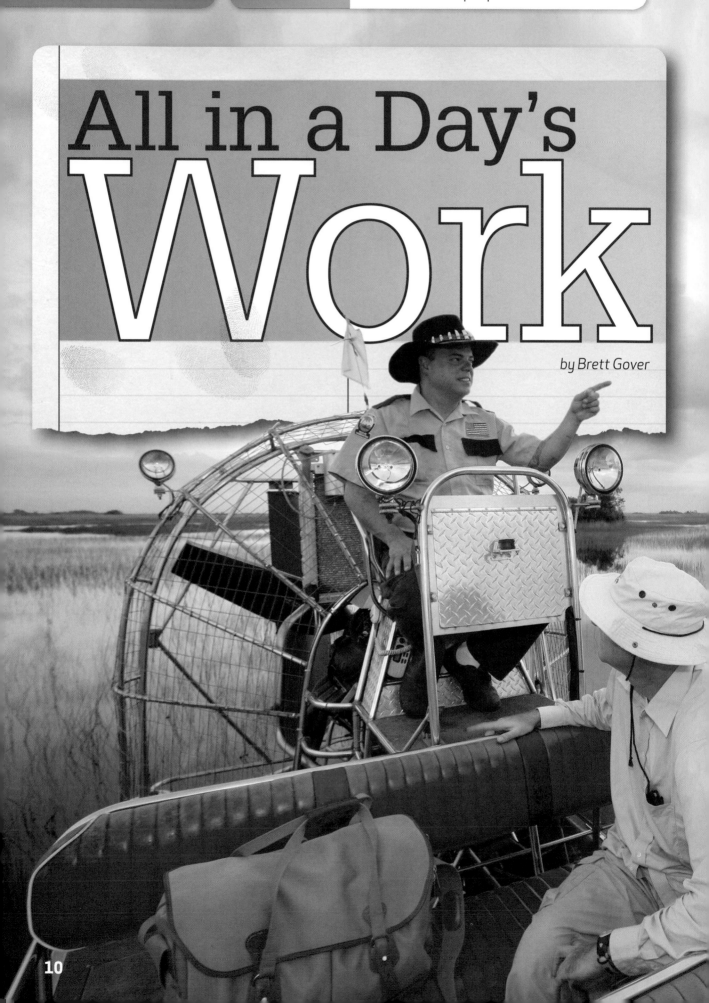

Many people choose to live on the Gulf Coast because of its warm weather, diverse wildlife, and beautiful beaches. But people here have to work, too, and the Gulf Coast offers many jobs.

First, let's look at jobs on the water. Ships travel on the Gulf and on rivers and canals, delivering goods to many harbors. There are many jobs on the ships and docks, loading and unloading goods.

Underneath the water, workers drill to reach oil. We use oil to fuel cars and heat homes. Oil is in other products, too, such as paint and even toothpaste.

Many people work in the fishing industry. Millions of fish live in the Gulf of Mexico. Without Gulf Coast seafood, much of the country wouldn't have oysters and shrimp.

Don't forget tourism. Every year, millions of people visit the Gulf Coast to enjoy beaches, underwater marvels, and wildlife. That creates a lot of jobs.

A ranger glides in an airboat through the Everglades. The Everglades is a swamp at the southern tip of Florida. It makes up the eastern edge of the Gulf Coast.

Trawling for Shrimp

Hi! I'm Jackie. I'm out shrimping on my Uncle Mick's trawler, a boat that drags **trawls**, or huge nets, along the seafloor. A large trawler can catch thousands of pounds of shrimp in one day.

5:00 A.M. As we chug-chug out of the harbor, I help Uncle Mick check the boat's ropes, pulleys, anchors, and nets.

6:30 A.M. Uncle Mick hauls up his first catch of shrimp. We pack the squiggly shrimp on ice. They look like huge insects. Uncle Mick sees a shark circling the boat, attracted to our bait.

10:00 A.M. The shark's gone, but storm clouds head in. Storms can bring waves strong enough to tip our trawler. We cruise back to the harbor to wait out the bad weather.

2:00 P.M. We're back on the water after the storm, and Uncle Mick asks me to fix a tear in the netting. I wonder if the shark did this.

4:00 P.M. We haul up the last catch. We head to port, where we'll sell the catch. Then we go home for dinner. After so much shrimp, we're ready for cheeseburgers.

Smaller shrimp boats like this one are best for fishing in shallow water.

13

These workers are drilling for oil on a rig. Workers on a rig need to wear helmets and goggles when doing this dangerous job.

Drilling for Oil on the Seafloor

I'm Jerry. I work on an oil rig in the ocean. A rig is a platform where oil is gathered from beneath the seafloor. The rig is far out at sea, so we work here for weeks at a time. A large rig has a cafeteria, a theater, a gym, and a store—not that we get much free time. We work 12-hour shifts, and the work is dangerous.

6:00 A.M. It's meeting time! Managers discuss how to keep oil flowing and keep workers safe. The oil from one rig might bring in more than a billion dollars a year. We work to avoid mistakes because oil spills hurt the environment, waste oil, and cost money. But they are always a danger with the complex machines we use.

7:00 A.M. to 7:00 P.M. First, we check our instruments, make repairs, and move equipment into place. The danger of explosions is on our minds as we handle huge machines. The oil comes up through pipes and into a tank. Then workers pump it into a ship, which takes it to be processed. The rig operates all day, as new workers sign on when we sign off. After dinner, I'll call my family, and then read a book.

Many trainers have studied
biology and animal behavior.

Training Dolphins

I'm Morgan, a dolphin trainer at a Gulf Coast marine park. Some people think dolphins shouldn't be used for entertainment. Lots of groups rescue injured dolphins. They nurse them to health and release them. But most dolphins in parks such as ours were born here. Trainers work to keep the dolphins healthy and happy.

6:30 A.M. to Noon Time to "bucket it out" for the morning meal. A dolphin gobbles as many as 20 pounds of fish a day! I swim with the dolphins and keep them learning with hand signals, whistles, and treats. Whenever a dolphin does something cool, I throw it a fish. That's an effective training technique for these intelligent mammals.

1:00 P.M. After noontime feeding comes the dolphin show! The dolphins show the audience how smart they are. I give a hand signal, and two dolphins swim, jump and flip together, and make a splash. People close by get wet, but they don't mind.

3:00 P.M. My shift is over, but I take notes on what I've learned. I note the dolphins' moods, new noises, and appearance. I talk to our scientists and doctors about the dolphins. I'm lucky to work so closely with these marine mammals.

Check In What kinds of jobs do people have in the Gulf Coast region?

Oil, Oil EVERYWHERE!

by Stuart Ewell

∧ Can you see any oil products in this picture? Oil was used to make the road. The skateboarder's helmet and the skateboard's wheels are made of oil as well.

Oil is a very important fuel. Oil and the products that come from it help us heat our homes and power our cars. It's also used to make products like cameras and tennis rackets. But sometimes oil can create problems. Oil spills **pollute**, or poison, the places where many plants and animals live. Burning oil as a fuel can harm the atmosphere, or the blanket of air that covers Earth.

Oil is found deep beneath the ground. It collects in large pools, called **reserves**. Maybe you've seen cartoons that show characters digging into the ground until black liquid suddenly shoots up. They make finding and collecting oil look easy, but we know it's not that simple.

1. Hundreds of millions of years ago, tiny bits of dead plants and animals (shown in brown and green above) were buried beneath mud (gray). Some bits were buried under the ocean (blue), some were not.
2. Over time, heat and pressure turned some of the mud into heavy rock. This rock layer (dark brown) pressed down on the layer of dead plants and animals.
3. The immense pressure turned the plants and animals into oil (black) and other fuels we collect from below the ocean's floor today.

Drilling in the Sea

Imagine drinking orange juice out of a straw. To drink the juice, you add suction, or pressure, on the straw. We get oil from underground in a similar way. Oil drillers use an engine to create pressure that sucks the oil up a pipe to Earth's surface.

The easiest way to get oil is to dig in the ground. That's where companies began looking for oil reserves. But after 150 years of collecting oil, the oil under land is harder to find. Scientists have started looking under the ocean floor.

Oil companies use **derricks** to extract oil from under the sea. A derrick looks like a tower on a platform. Derricks are built above the ocean floor where oil has been found. Pulleys and cables attached to the derrick move huge drills into the ocean floor. Then the oil is pumped up to the derrick, where it is placed in tanks.

This huge oil rig is located along the Gulf Coast. It is near Port Aransas, Texas.

PRO: It Makes Our World Run

We mainly use oil to fuel our cars and to heat our homes. But we need oil for other things, too. We use oil to make electricity. It powers refrigerators and ovens. Oil also powers the pump that brings water to our houses and the machine that heats our water.

Plastic building blocks are made from oil products.

Want to wash your hair or play outside? Your shampoo and your soccer ball might have been made with oil products. Anything plastic has oil in it. Even the soles of your shoes may be made with oil.

Imagine how long it would take to walk as far as a car can travel in one hour. Imagine the number of people it would take to build a building without modern machines that run on fuel made from oil.

We count on oil products every day. We are **dependent** on them. The more oil we use to make products, the more oil we need to find. So, until we learn to use less of it, or find other fuel options, we'll keep drilling.

Gas made from oil powers lawn mowers. Their tires are also made from oil products.

People use oil to build the parts of a car. Oil powers cars, too.

Industrial oil is used to make gasoline.

Most basketballs are made with oil.

CON: Stop the Drilling!

While oil is very useful, drilling for it in the Gulf of Mexico is dangerous. Workers have to be highly skilled and follow safety rules to prevent accidents. Even so, explosions on oil rigs have injured and killed workers. Oil spills have polluted our waters and killed countless animals.

In April 2010, 11 workers died from an explosion on the oil derrick *Deepwater Horizon*. It spilled thousands of gallons of oil into the Gulf. It took five months to seal the leak and stop the flow. Chemicals were used to pull oil out of the water. But oil still washed up onto beaches, killing plants and animals. The Gulf is still recovering.

The oil spill affected the Gulf in many ways. Many fish died, which hurt the environment and the fishing economy. Tourism also went down. Fewer people visited, because they couldn't sunbathe on oil-covered beaches. When people didn't come, restaurants and hotels closed. Many people lost their jobs.

Oil makes people's lives better in many ways, but drilling for oil can also make life worse. We need oil, but we don't want it to keep polluting our waters and destroying habitats, or places where plants and animals live. As oil becomes harder to find, we will have to find other sources of power. Let's start now.

When oil spills, volunteers help clean up by shoveling oily sand off beaches. Workers clean the feathers of birds in this picture. The birds have been coated in oil from the Gulf oil spill.

Check In | What are some products in your home that are made with oil?

Deadly Winds

by Elizabeth Massie

This painting is an artist's depiction of the destruction Galveston suffered during the 1900 hurricane.

Winds scream and rain slams the ground. Trees fall and waves crash onto land. What's happening? It's a **hurricane**.

The Gulf Coast region has lots of storms. The Gulf's warm, moist air meets cooler air from the north. The warm water whips the cooler air into strong winds. The winds spin faster into a hurricane. Many hurricanes have pounded the Gulf region.

In 1900, a hurricane hit Galveston, Texas. This island city next to the Gulf was home to more than 35,000 people. On September 8, 1900, this hurricane killed about 6,000 people and damaged the city.

The Weather Bureau warned Galveston that a storm was coming. But back then, forecasters couldn't tell how powerful a storm would be or where it would hit.

Flags went up in the harbor to warn people, but locals had lived through many storms and weren't afraid. Powerful winds knocked down electrical wires and caused flooding when the hurricane struck. The director of the Galveston Weather Office later wrote:

This map shows the path the hurricane of 1900 took.

I reached home and found the water around my residence waist deep. I at once went to work assisting people . . . into my residence. . . . By 8 p.m. a number of houses had drifted up and lodged to the east and southeast of my residence, and these with the force of the waves acted as a battering ram . . . and at 8:30 p.m. my residence went down with about fifty persons who had sought it for safety.

The Deadly Storm Strikes

Violent winds pushed water over the island. Some buildings were torn apart and others were flattened. **Debris**, or scattered remains of objects, filled the area.

Milton Elford and his family left their home and hurried to a larger house nearby. Their house could not withstand the storm. Milton survived but his family did not. Later, he wrote:

> We all gathered in one room; all at once the house went from its foundation and the water came in waist-deep, and we all made a break for the door, but could not get it open. We then smashed out the window and I led the way. I had only got part way out when the house fell on us. I was hit on the head with something and it knocked me out and into the water head first. . . . I came up and got hold of some wreckage on the other side of the house.

Samuel Young watched the storm first from the beach. Then he watched from the wharf, where ships land. He described what he saw:

> The debris fairly flew past, so rapid had the tide become. At twenty minutes to six o'clock . . . there was a marked increase in the violence of the wind. . . . I saw the tide rise fully four feet in one bound. In a few minutes several houses . . . went to pieces and floated away.

At first, Ida Smith Austin wasn't too concerned about the approaching storm. Her opinion soon changed:

> The wind seemed to grow more furious reaching the incredible velocity [force] of 120 miles an hour. Blinds were torn off windows, frames, sash and all, blown in, and the rainwater stood an inch and a half on upstairs floors.

The Galveston hurricane destroyed more than 2,500 homes. Buildings were knocked down by strong winds and pounding waves. The water rose as high as 15 to 20 feet.

WE DON'T LIKE IKE

GOD BLESS GALVESTON

Many houses along the Gulf Coast are built on stilts. This one is boarded up as Hurricane Ike approaches.

After the Storm

People across America helped the survivors of Galveston. Some sent money, and others traveled there to help clean up the city. Clara Barton, the founder of the Red Cross, arrived on September 17, 1900. She and others gave out food and clothes.

Engineers designed a 17-foot-high seawall to stop future waves from hitting the shore. That seawall still stands today. They also raised the island's land in some areas. These improvements helped when Hurricane Ike hit the island in 2008. Though that hurricane **devastated** Galveston, early warnings allowed many people to leave the city safely. About 74 people died in Hurricane Ike, compared with the thousands who died in 1900.

Hurricanes cannot be stopped, but meteorologists can keep an eye on them. The National Hurricane Center uses airplanes and satellites to track hurricanes. The planes and satellites allow them to predict storms earlier. People can be warned to leave an area before the deadly winds strike.

Check In How did the people of Galveston make it a safer city after the hurricane?

Discuss

1. What connections can you make among the five selections in this book? How are the selections related?

2. How are people who live on the Gulf Coast affected by the water and land around them?

3. What are the advantages and disadvantages of drilling for oil in the Gulf?

4. Compare the hurricanes that hit Galveston in 1900 and 2008. How did changes in weather forecasting technology affect how people weathered each storm?

5. What do you still wonder about the Gulf Coast? How can you learn more?